Let's Learn About… Cats!

Curious Toddler Series

Volume 2

Cheryl Shireman

ISBN: 1477533737
ISBN-13: 978-1477533734

DEDICATION

This book is dedicated to Anna Lee - my favorite toddler.

With much love, Bomb Bomb

Some cats sleep on their belly.

Some sleep on their back.

Baby cats are called kittens.

Kittens grow up into adult cats.

Some cats are one color.

Some cats are two colors, or even more!

Cats like to nap.

Cats like to hide.

Some cats have short hair.

Some cats have long hair.

Kittens are born in groups
called litters.

Many brothers and sisters can
be born in one litter.

Some cats like to relax.

Some cats like to play!

Cats depend on us to feed and
water them.

Cats give themselves a bath by licking their fur.

Some cats like to crawl over
things.

Some cats like to crawl under
things.

Cat's feet are called paws.
Cats have claws on all four feet.

Cats have special claws that
help them to climb.

Some cats like to explore.

Some cats like to cuddle
instead.

Cats like to play with strings.

Cats like to chase things!

Some cats have green eyes.

Some cats have blue eyes.

When a cat is mad it makes a
sound called hissing.

When a cat is happy it makes
a sound called purring.

And the very best place for a
purring kitty,

is on your lap!

 The end.

We hope you enjoyed this
Curious Toddler book.

Also in the Curious Toddler series...

Let's Learn About...Dogs!
Let's Learn About...Cats!
Let's Learn About...Things to Drive!
Let's Learn About...Jungle Animals!
Let's Learn About...Birds!
Let's Learn About...Wild Animals!
Let's Learn About...Horses!
Let's Learn About...Farm Animals!

Let's Learn About ...
DOGS !
A CURIOUS TODDLER BOOK
Ages 2-5
Volume 1
Cheryl Shireman

Let's Learn About ...
CATS !
A CURIOUS TODDLER BOOK
Ages 2-5
Volume 2
Cheryl Shireman

Let's Learn About ...
Things to DRIVE !
A CURIOUS TODDLER BOOK
Ages 2-5
Volume 3
Cheryl Shireman

Let's Learn About ...
JUNGLE ANIMALS!
A CURIOUS TODDLER BOOK
Ages 2-5
Volume 4
Cheryl Shireman

Let's Learn About ...
BIRDS!
A CURIOUS TODDLER BOOK
Ages 2-5
Volume 5
Cheryl Shireman

Let's Learn About ...
WILD ANIMALS!
A CURIOUS TODDLER BOOK
Ages 2-5
Volume 6
Cheryl Shireman

Let's Learn About ...
HORSES!
A CURIOUS TODDLER BOOK
Ages 2-5
Volume 7
Cheryl Shireman

Let's Learn About ...
FARM ANIMALS!
A CURIOUS TODDLER BOOK
Ages 2-5
Volume 8
Cheryl Shireman

ABOUT THE AUTHOR

Cheryl Shireman created the Curious Toddler Series. Cheryl is married and lives in Indiana on a beautiful lake with her husband. She has three grown children and one adorable granddaughter.

Cheryl also writes novels for big people:
Life is But a Dream: On The Lake
Life is But a Dream: In The Mountains
Broken Resolutions
Cooper Moon: The Calling

She is also the author of the beloved non-fiction book, You Don't Need a Prince: A Letter to My Daughter

All of her books can be found online on Amazon.
Her website is www.cherylshireman.com
She can also be found on Twitter and Facebook.

Printed in Great Britain
by Amazon

86062757R00025